DEC 0 5 1997

A ROOKIE BIOGRAPHY

JOHANN SEBASTIAN BACH

Great Man of Music

By Carol Greene

CHILDRENS PRESS®

CHICAGO

This book is for Norma Sauer.

Johann Sebastian Bach (1685-1750)

Library of Congress Cataloging-in-Publication Data

Greene, Carol.
    Johann Sebastian Bach, great man of music / by Carol Greene.
      p. cm. — (A Rookie biography)
    Includes index.
    Summary: A biography of the prolific eighteenth-century composer
and organist who created some of the world's greatest instrumental and
religious music.
    ISBN 0-516-04251-3
    1. Bach, Johann Sebastian, 1685-1750—Juvenile literature.
    2. Composers—Germany—Biography—Juvenile literature. [1. Bach,
Johann Sebastian, 1685-1750. 2. Composers.] I. Title. II. Series: Greene,
Carol. Rookie biography.
ML3930.B2G73   1992
780'.92—dc20
[B]
                                              92-7373
                                              CIP
                                         AC MN

Johann Sebastian Bach
was a real person.
He was born in 1685.
He died in 1750.
Bach was one of
the greatest musicians
who ever lived.
This is his story.

TABLE OF CONTENTS

Chapter 1

A Musical Family

Johann Sebastian Bach
had to make music.

His great-grandfather
played the violin.
So did his grandfather.
Dozens of uncles and cousins
all made music.

His father played
many instruments—and he sang.
His big brothers
took music lessons.
So Johann Sebastian Bach
had to make music.

He loved it.

Johann Sebastian Bach was born in this house in Eisenach, Germany.
The family gathered to play music in the living room (below).

Left: The town of Eisenach today. Below: Johann Sebastian Bach's violin

At home in the town of Eisenach, Germany, his father taught him to play the violin. He studied at school and sang at church.

Then, when Johann Sebastian
was only ten,
his mother and father died.
His grown-up brother,
Johann Christoph, took
Johann Sebastian to his house.

Johann Christoph could play
the organ and the clavier.
(A clavier is like a piano.)
He taught Johann Sebastian
to play them too.

Johann Sebastian learned fast.
He kept asking for
harder and harder music.

His brother kept a book
of hard music
in a locked cabinet.
He said the music was too
hard for Johann Sebastian.

But late at night,
Johann Sebastian went
to that cabinet.
He put his hand
through a hole
and pulled out the music.

He copied the whole book
by the light of the stars.
It took him six months.

Then Johann Christoph
found the copy.
He took it away.
Poor Johann Sebastian!

When he was fifteen,
Johann Sebastian heard
about St. Michael's School
in the town of Lüneburg.
Poor boys who were good
at music could go there free.

The town of Lüneburg, Germany

That was the place
for Johann Sebastian.
Off he went.
He and a friend
walked all the way
—over 150 miles.

Bach studied very hard in school.
And he often walked many miles
to hear famous musicians play.

Johann Sebastian
studied hard at
St. Michael's.
He learned
Greek, Latin,
religion, poetry,
and all kinds
of music.
He played
instruments
and sang, too.

Then, when he was seventeen,
Johann Sebastian
left St. Michael's.
Now he had to find a job
making music.

12

Chapter 2

That Amazing Bach

For a while, Bach played violin in an orchestra in the town of Weimar. Then he got a better job playing the organ at the New Church in Arnstadt.

Bach was organist at the church at Arnstadt.

Bach played beautiful music.
But the church board said
he made his music too hard.
People couldn't sing to it.
Bach didn't like that.

Inside a church in Arnstadt

The board also asked him
to start a boys' choir.
The boys were brats.
They couldn't sing, either.
Bach didn't like them.

He did like a girl
he met in Arnstadt.
Her name was Maria Barbara.
Bach liked her very much.

At last he asked the board
for four weeks off.
He wanted to hear
Dietrich Buxtehude,
a great organist
in another town.
The board said yes.

But Bach didn't stay four weeks.
He stayed four months.
He learned many things
from old Buxtehude.

Soon he quit his job
at Arnstadt and took
a job at Mühlhausen.
But he couldn't leave
Maria Barbara behind.
So they got married.

Bach had been writing
music for some time.
At Mühlhausen he began
to write much more.

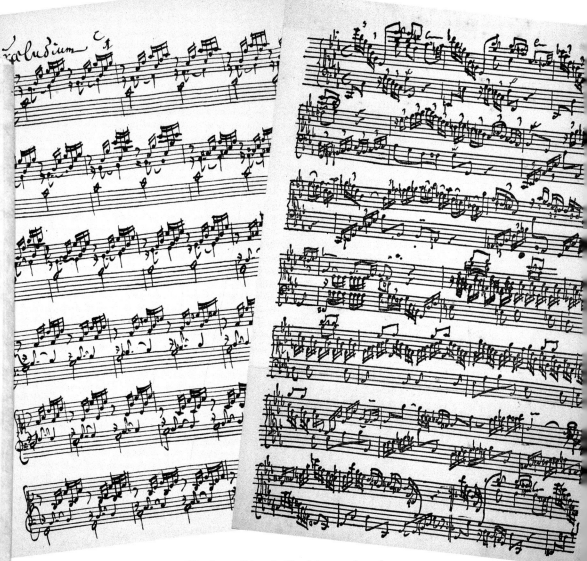

Music written in Bach's own hand

He wrote fine organ music.
He wrote cantatas
—long pieces for singers,
organ, and an orchestra, too.

Before long,
Duke Wilhelm
asked Bach to come
back to Weimar
and be the
court organist.
Bach went.

Duke Wilhelm (left) asked
Bach to come to the town
of Weimar, Germany (below).

This statue of Johann Sebastian Bach in Leipzig
is one of many Bach statues found in Germany.

At Weimar, he kept writing.
But it was his playing
that made him famous.
Bach could play *anything*.

Someone said that once
he couldn't reach a note
with his fingers.
So he used a stick
held between his teeth.

Someone else said
he once played a note
with his nose!

Bach could sit at the organ
and make up hard music
while he was playing.

He's amazing! people said.

Prince Leopold of Anhalt-Cöthen

Chapter 3

Changes

One day, Prince Leopold
of Anhalt-Cöthen visited Weimar.
He heard Bach play
and made up his mind.
Soon he asked Bach
to come work for him.

Bach was ready to go.
But Duke Wilhelm said no.
Bach must work for *him*.
Bach kept asking to leave
until the duke got mad.
He had Bach put in jail.

Johann Sebastian Bach in 1715

But that didn't bother Bach.
He just picked up his pen
and wrote more music.

At last the duke gave up.
So Bach packed his music,
gathered his family,
and set out for Leopold's
court at Anhalt-Cöthen.

What a change from Weimar!
Duke Wilhelm had been gloomy.
Prince Leopold was happy.
He loved music, and
he loved Bach.

A musical performance during the time Bach lived, featuring an organist, a conductor, and an orchestra

Churches in Anhalt-Cöthen
didn't use much music.
So Bach wrote for
small groups of instruments.
He played in the groups, too.

One day, Prince Leopold
took Bach on a trip.
When they got back,
Bach learned that his wife,
Maria Barbara, had died.

Bach and the four children
missed her very much.
Bach began to wish he could
write church music again.
That might help him
feel a little better.

Then he fell in love
with Anna Magdalena.
Anna loved birds, flowers,
music, children, and Bach.

They got married, and
she soon made the Bach home
a happy place again.

Prince Leopold got married, too.
But his new wife was stingy.
She didn't like to
spend money for music.

In Bach's time, men wore big, curly wigs.

Time for a new job,
thought Bach.
Maybe it should be
a job making church music.

Leipzig, Germany, as it looks today.
Inset: St. Thomas Church

Chapter 4

A Big Job

Leipzig was a big city.
St. Thomas was a big church.
When they needed
a new music director,
Bach asked for the job.
He got it.

Now he'd make church music
and music for the city, too.
That sounded perfect to Bach.
But it wasn't.

Inside St. Thomas Church, the organ is seen at the center of the picture.

Bach playing the organ with the church choir in Leipzig

He had to work too hard.
He even had to teach boys
at St. Thomas School.
Crabby people bossed him.
And he didn't make much money.

He and Anna had
thirteen children in Leipzig.
Seven died while they
were still small.
That was very hard.

But when Bach felt sad,
he and his family would
make music together.
Then they all felt better.

Bach playing music with his wife and children

Sometimes Bach wanted
to leave Leipzig.
He wanted an easier job
with nice people
and more pay.

But he never left.
And in spite of all
the bad things, he wrote
some of the most beautiful
music in the world.

A painting of Bach, and the first
page of the music for the *St. Matthew Passion*

The *St. Matthew Passion*
and the *B-Minor Mass*
sound like music from heaven.
But Johann Sebastian Bach
wrote them right there
in Leipzig.

Johann Sebastian Bach (bottom right) with three of his sons
(clockwise from top left): Carl, Wilhelm, Johann Christian

Chapter 5

Last Years

As Bach grew older,
he saw that young musicians
would not write music like his.
They liked different music.

Four of Bach's own sons
—Carl, Wilhelm, Friedrich,
and Johann Christian—
became famous musicians.
But they were not
like their father.

So Bach made his music
as perfect as he could.
That was his gift
to God and to the world.

One day, he met
King Frederick
the Great. The
king played a
simple tune
for him. Bach
turned the tune
into difficult
music. The
king loved it.

King Frederick the Great

King Frederick the Great (right) loved Bach's music.

When Bach got home,
he turned the tune
into a great piece.
He called it *Musical Offering*
and gave it to the king.

Bach's eyes had been bad
for a long time.
Now he became blind.
An operation didn't help.

But Bach still wanted
to write more music.
So he told his son-in-law
what to write down for him.

That is how Bach
wrote his last piece.
It is like a hymn.
The words begin:
"Before Your throne,
my God, I stand."

Bach had felt close
to God all his life.
He had never been
afraid of dying.

Anna and the children
were around his bed
on July 28, 1750,
when Bach did go
to stand before God's throne.
He was sixty-five years old.

Students playing Bach's music on recorders
at the foot of his statue in Leipzig

Back then, people knew
Bach was a great musician.
But they didn't understand
that the music he wrote
was great, too.

It took almost 100 years
for the world to see
what treasures it had from
Johann Sebastian Bach.

Important Dates

1685   March 21—Born in Eisenach, Germany, to Elisabeth and Johann Ambrosius Bach

1700   Went to St. Michael's School, Lüneburg

1703   Played in orchestra at Weimar
Became organist at New Church, Arnstadt

1707   Became organist at St. Blasius Church, Mühlhausen
Married Maria Barbara

1708   Became court organist to Duke Wilhelm Ernst in Weimar

1717   Joined court of Prince Leopold at Anhalt-Cöthen

1720   Maria Barbara died

1721   Married Anna Magdalena

1723   Became musical director at St. Thomas Church, Leipzig

1750   July 28—Died in Leipzig, Germany

INDEX

Page numbers in boldface type indicate illustrations.

PHOTO CREDITS

ABOUT THE AUTHOR

Carol Greene has degrees in English literature and musicology. She has worked in international exchange programs, as an editor, and as a teacher of writing. She now lives in Webster Groves, Missouri, and writes full-time. She has published more than 100 books, including those in the Rookie Biographies series.